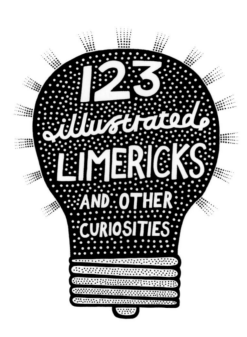

123 illustrated LIMERICKS AND OTHER CURIOSITIES

HÓTEL
LEIFUR EIRÍKSSON

ALL
THAT WE'VE GOT IS
THIS PALE BLUE DOT

DANCE
LIKE THERE'S NO
TOMORROW

ANGRY DAN

IF EVERY FORCE CAN RELY
ON AN EQUAL OPPOSING REPLY
DID PLANET EARTH BOUNCE
BY EQUAL AMOUNTS
WHEN THE
APPLE
FELL OUT OF
THE SKY?

I FIND YOUR ALLURE SO
APPEALING
MY POOR LITTLE
HEART'S HIT WITH DESIRE
DUMBSTRUCK WITH DESIRE
I DARE NOT ENQUIRE IF IT
MIGHT BE A MUTUAL
FEELING

TURNER'S
MOST FORMATIVE TIMES
IN OUR GLORIOUS CUMBRIAN CLIMES
WOULD ENSURE HIS CONVICTIONS
AND LATTER DEPICTIONS
OF THE GRANDEUR OF
NATURE'S SUBLIME

JAMES STARLEY
REVEALS A VISION
OF LIFE ON TWO WHEELS
THE PEOPLE-ALIKE-CAN ALL
RIDE A BIKE AND SOON WE'LL
BE HEAD OVER HEELS

JAMES STARLEY · INVENTOR · 1830-1881
FATHER OF THE BICYCLE INDUSTRY

THERE
ARE
PEOPLE
WHOM
ALL WILL
ADORE
WITH A
SWEETNESS
THAT'S HARD
TO IGNORE...

AND
THEN
SOME
WHO REVEAL A
PERPLEXING APPEAL
JUST
TO
THOSE
WHO SEEK OUT THEIR
ALLURE

ANGRY DAN

A CANTANKEROUS
MAN FROM CARLISLE
SOLD LIQUORICE LACE BY THE MILE
I SAID "THAT'S ECCENTRIC
WHY DON'T YOU GO METRIC?"
HE SAID "KILOMETRES
AIN'T WORTH MY WHILE"

JOHN RUSKIN
INSPIRED BY THIS LAND
DECLARED HIS COMPELLING DEMAND
A WORLD FILLED WITH BEAUTY IS
EACH PERSON'S DUTY IN AS MUCH
AS OUR MEANS WILL COMMAND

ANGRY DAN

EVERY ARTIST
WILL LIKELY IMPART
THERE'S ONE SIMPLE WAY TO
MAKE ART
TAKE YOURSELF TO A PLACE
WHERE YOU'VE TIME AND SOME SPACE
AND THEN (HERE'S THE
IMPORTANT BIT) ... START.

DECIDE WHO YOU'D
LIKE TO BECOME
WITHOUT CARE FOR
WHAT OTHERS HAVE DONE
LET YOUR PURPOSE BEGIN
FROM A PLACE DEEP WITHIN
GUIDED BY THE BEAT OF YOUR OWN DRUM

ANGRY DAN

A CANTANKEROUS
MAN FROM CARLISLE
SOLD LIQUORICE LACE BY THE MILE
I SAID "THAT'S ECCENTRIC
WHY DON'T YOU GO METRIC?"
HE SAID "KILOMETRES
AIN'T WORTH MY WHILE"

TODO LO
QUE TENEMOS ES ESTE
PÁLIDO PUNTO AZUL.

BE CAREFUL OF
THOSE WHO COMPOSE WITH
COLLECTIVE NOUNS
IN THEIR PROSE YOU'LL SOON BE
SWEPT UP IN A LITTER OF PUPS
OR KILLED BY A
MURDER OF CROWS

EVERY ARTIST WILL LIKELY IMPART
THAT THERE'S ONE SIMPLE WAY TO
MAKE ART
TAKE YOURSELF TO A PLACE
WHERE YOU'VE TIME AND SOME SPACE
AND THEN (HERE'S THE IMPORTANT BIT) START.

THE STRANGE
ILLUSTRATOR WITHIN
LIES AWAKE THROUGH
THE NIGHT WITH A GRIN
AND HE DRAWS WHAT HE THINKS IN
INVISIBLE INKS
THEN THROWS IT ALL
INTO THE BIN

ANGRY DAN

WORDSWORTH
RECOUNTED A SCENE
OF A JOURNEY THROUGH CUMBRIAN GREEN
HIS WHIMSICAL SIGHT
OF SOME FLOWERS SO BRIGHT
WOULD DEFINE ALL OF ENGLAND'S SERENE

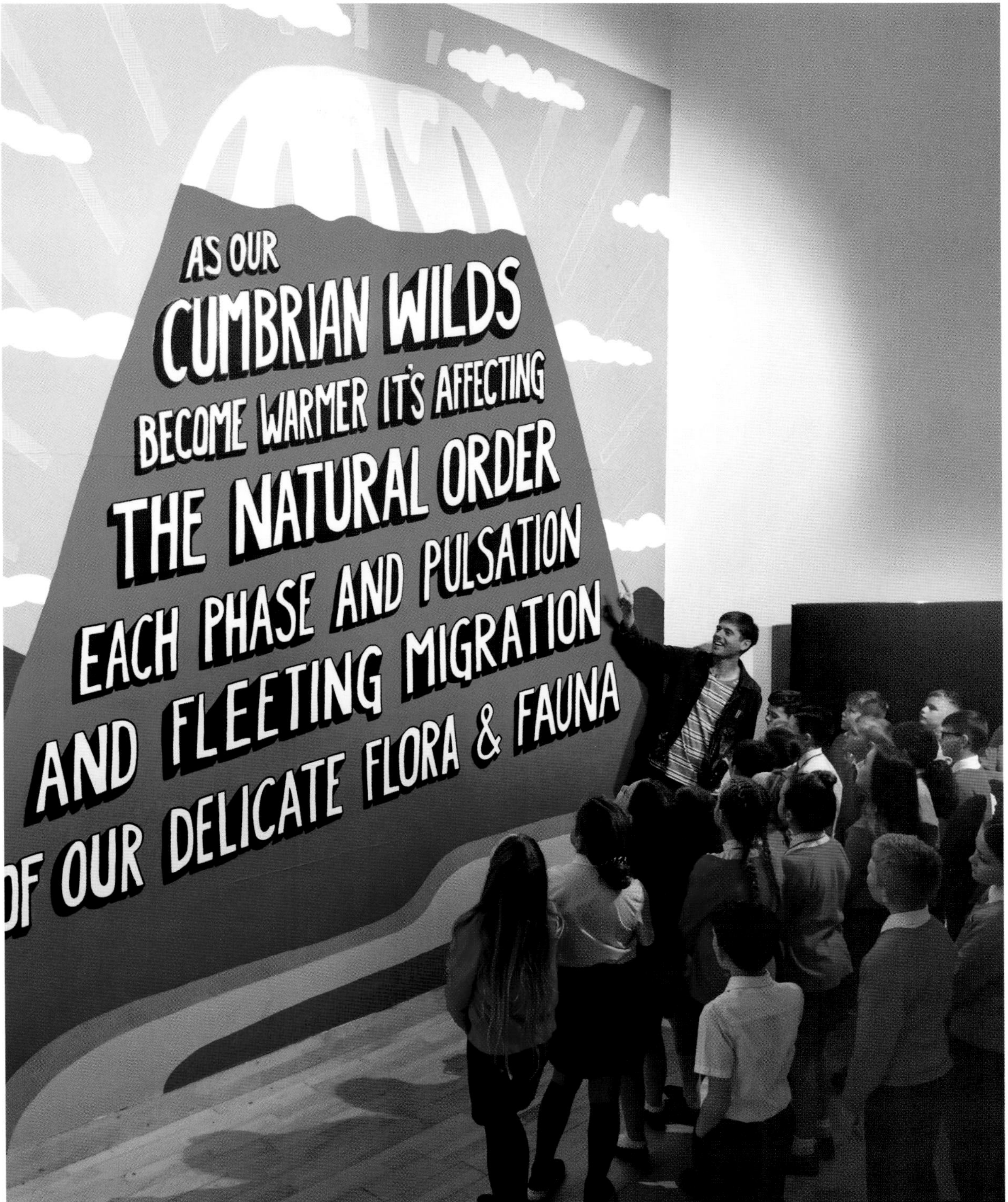

AS OUR
CUMBRIAN WILDS
BECOME WARMER IT'S AFFECTING
THE NATURAL ORDER
EACH PHASE AND PULSATION
AND FLEETING MIGRATION
OF OUR DELICATE FLORA & FAUNA

About Me

I have spent the last 7 years writing limericks, illustrating them in bright colours, and painting them on the street.

In 2019, I was commissioned by the Mayor's London Borough of Culture to paint 9 limerick murals in Waltham Forest, creating a treasure hunt of my work. Since then, I have painted in towns and cities across the UK and overseas.

I have made two short films based on my rhyming monologues, an educational film about illustrated poetry for BBC Teach, and a show for Soho Radio about the history and culture of limericks.

In 2024, I drew a map of London's cultural landmarks. A 5000 square ft. version of the map was installed in the Queen Elizabeth Olympic Park for the opening weekend of London Mural Festival.

I work from my home studio in Walthamstow, London.

THE
LIMERICK
FORM
SO IT'S RECKONED
HAS A FIRST LINE
THAT RHYMES
WITH THE SECOND
ON THE FOURTH AND THE THIRD
SOMETHING DIFFERENT IS HEARD
WHILE THE FIFTH RETURNS TO WHERE BECKONED

Introduction

The day before the first day I started writing limericks was the last day I remember being bored, because from then onward, whenever I've a moment spare, I always try to write one. I've written them on buses, trains, boats, and planes. I've written them on the sides of mountains and while swimming in the sea. I've written them in supermarket checkout queues and during important meetings. I've written plenty while lying awake in the middle of the night and I've written plenty more whilst sitting on the toilet. They are - and I say this without sarcasm – one of my most faithful companions.

Much has been said of what constitutes a good limerick, with many commentators decreeing that only the dirty ones are ever any good. Now, don't get me wrong, I enjoy a dirty limerick. However, I do think a limerick can be much more than that. This is not to say I approach them with a lofty pretentiousness. I have received no formal training in either writing or drawing - a trait which I'm sure is evident throughout - and it is with this in mind that, in addition to their individual merits, I believe this body of work amounts to a true representation of myself and, as such, a pure and righteous artistic opus, unabated by the shackles of institutional doctrine. Either that or it's just a bunch of stupid poems, but I'll let you be the judge...

CHAPTERS

Life Lessons

DECIDE WHO YOU'D LIKE TO BECOME WITHOUT CARE FOR WHAT OTHERS HAVE DONE LET YOUR PURPOSE BEGIN FROM A PLACE DEEP WITHIN DRIVEN BY THE BEAT OF YOUR OWN DRUM

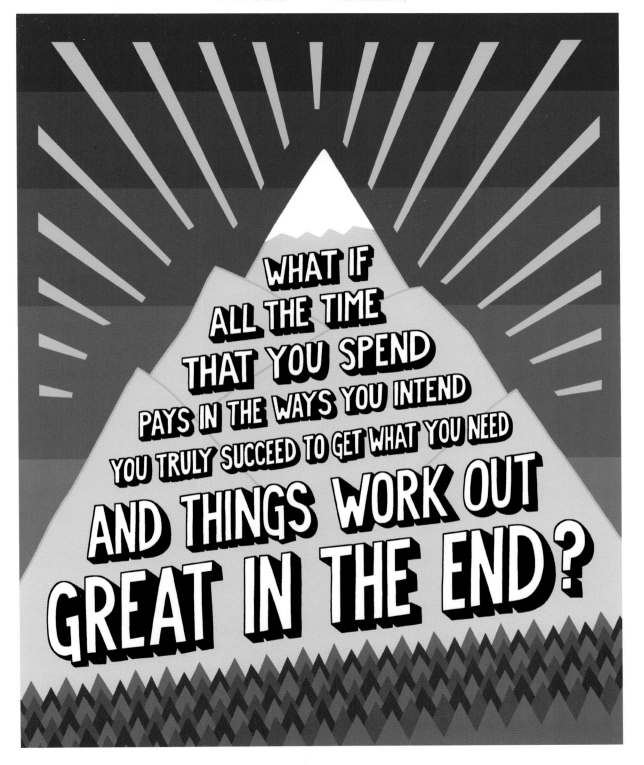

SIT UP STRAIGHT
BREATHE IN DEEP THROUGH YOUR NOSE
EXHALE AS YOUR EYES GENTLY CLOSE

BE SIMPLY AWARE

OF THE MOVEMENT OF AIR

AND THE CALM OF YOUR MIND AS IT SLOWS

REGARDLESS
HOW OFTEN IT SEEMS
OTHER PEOPLE MIGHT
KNOW WHAT LIFE MEANS
THE SOURCE OF YOUR PRIDE
IS FOR YOU TO DECIDE
SO YOU MIGHT AS WELL
FOLLOW YOUR DREAMS

BRUSHING YOUR TEETH
IS A CHORE
AND TO STAND ON ONE LEG IS A BORE.
QUITE AMUSING, HOWEVER, TO DO THEM TOGETHER,
AND IT'S GREAT FOR YOUR SMILE AND YOUR CORE.

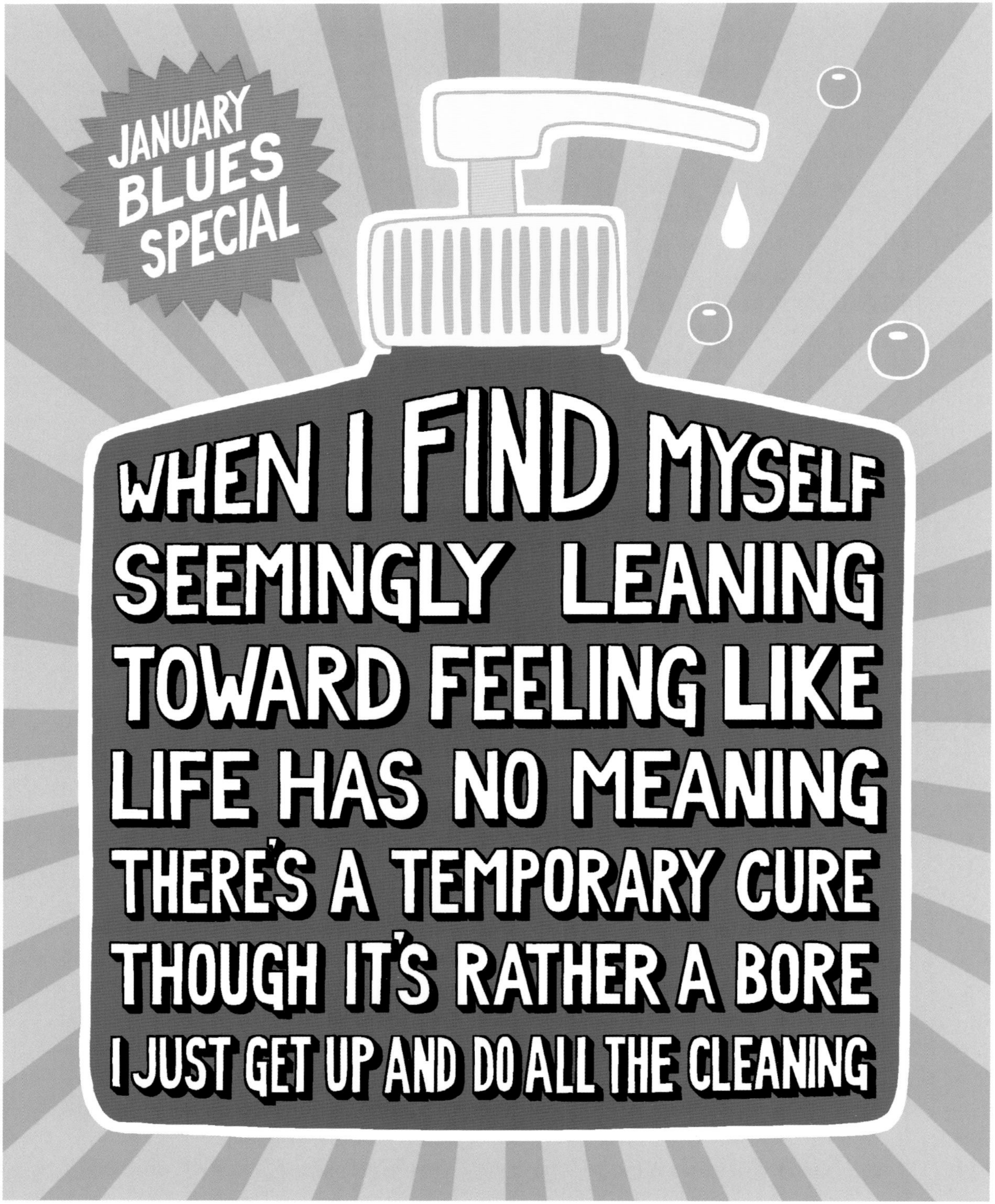
JANUARY BLUES SPECIAL
WHEN I FIND MYSELF
SEEMINGLY LEANING
TOWARD FEELING LIKE
LIFE HAS NO MEANING
THERE'S A TEMPORARY CURE
THOUGH IT'S RATHER A BORE
I JUST GET UP AND DO ALL THE CLEANING

IF YOU
LET YOURSELF BE DEFINED
BY HOW OTHER'S BELIEFS ARE ALIGNED
YOU MIGHT BE ALLOWED
TO BE ONE OF THE CROWD
BUT YOU'LL NEVER
BE ONE OF A
KIND

LET'S NOT MEASURE
OUR WORTH BY OUR PAY
OR OUR THOUGHTS
OR THE THINGS THAT WE SAY
OR OUR STATURE OR FAME
OR THE STRENGTH OF OUR NAME
BUT THE GOOD
THAT WE DO
WITH EACH DAY

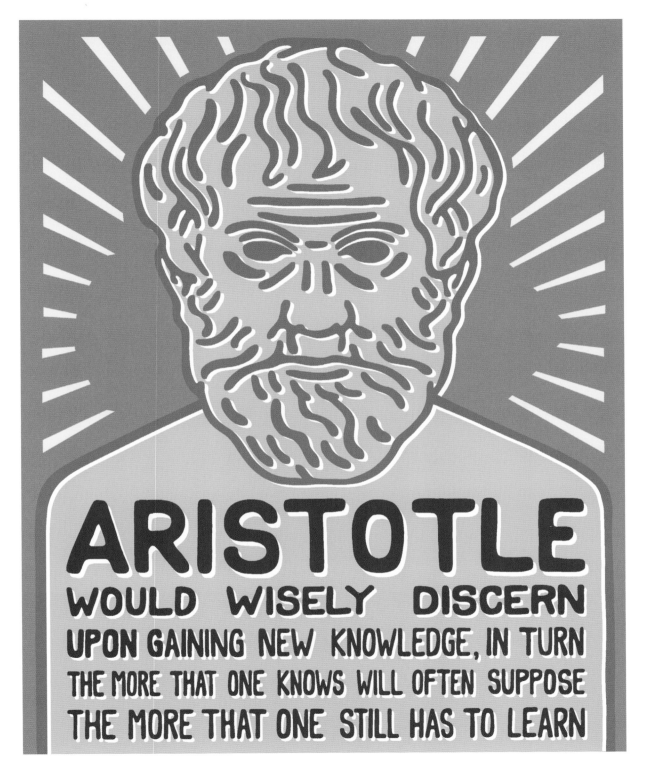

ARISTOTLE
WOULD WISELY DISCERN
UPON GAINING NEW KNOWLEDGE, IN TURN
THE MORE THAT ONE KNOWS WILL OFTEN SUPPOSE
THE MORE THAT ONE STILL HAS TO LEARN

DOES WISDOM DECREE THAT ONE OUGHT TO VALUE WHAT CANNOT BE TAUGHT BUT RATHER ATTAINED THROUGH WILLFUL, SUSTAINED ACTION AND RATIONAL THOUGHT?

BE BOLD AS YOU TRAVEL ALONG

THE PARTICULAR PATH THAT YOU'RE ON

YOU DON'T NEED TO EXPLAIN

YOUR INTENTIONS IN VAIN

TO THOSE WHO HAVE GOT YOU ALL WRONG

SOME DAYS
MY OLD BOTHERSOME BRAIN
SEEMS IMMERSED IN PAST HEARTACHES AND PAIN
'TIL A KIND AND SINCERE LITTLE VOICE IN MY EAR
HELPS ME FEEL LIKE MYSELF, ONCE AGAIN.

SAMARITANS 116 123

WHILE
THE FAITHFUL
SINCERELY PROPOSE
THERE'S A PLACE WHERE
OUR CONSCIOUSNESS GOES
NON-BELIEVERS INSIST THAT IT DOESN'T EXIST
BUT THE TRUTH IS THAT NOBODY KNOWS

31

YOUR TIME IS YOUR OWN TO INVEST IN THOSE **MEANINGFUL** WAYS YOU THINK BEST

YOU DON'T HAVE TO DO WHAT'S EXPECTED OF YOU IF IT'S JUST GOING TO MAKE YOU DEPRESSED

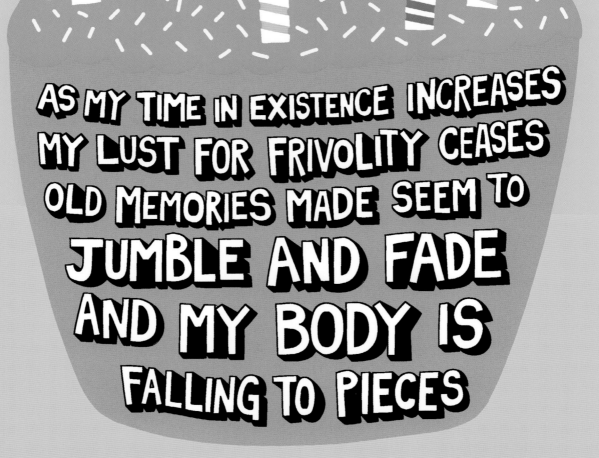

AS MY TIME IN EXISTENCE INCREASES
MY LUST FOR FRIVOLITY CEASES
OLD MEMORIES MADE SEEM TO
JUMBLE AND FADE
AND MY BODY IS
FALLING TO PIECES

WHEN HISTORY
EARNESTLY TELLS
OF HOW EVIL COLLUDES
AND COMPELS
WE SHOULD NOT DENY
WHAT THIS MIGHT IMPLY OF THE
DARKNESS INSIDE OF
OURSELVES.

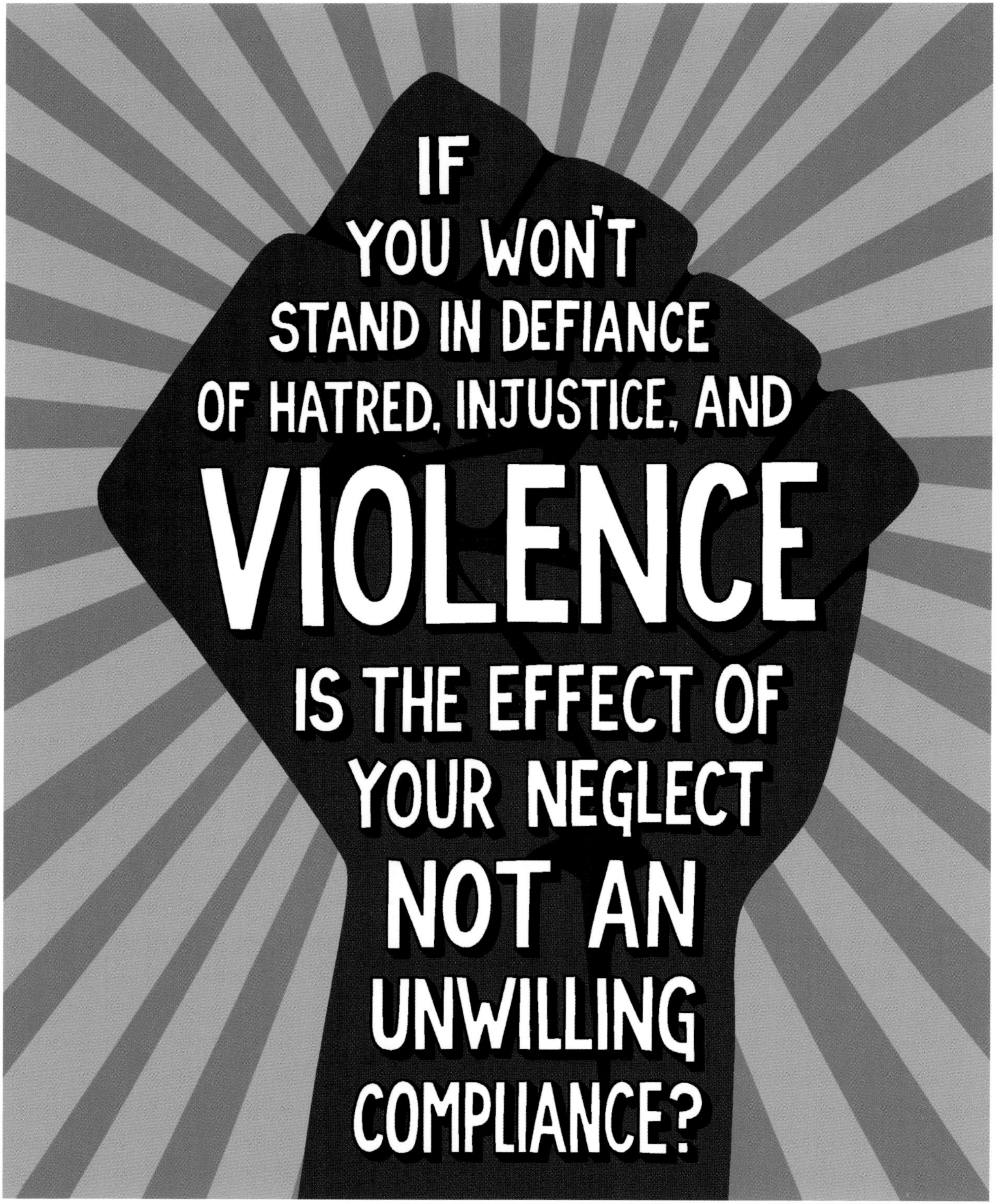
IF
YOU WON'T
STAND IN DEFIANCE
OF HATRED, INJUSTICE, AND
VIOLENCE
IS THE EFFECT OF
YOUR NEGLECT
NOT AN
UNWILLING
COMPLIANCE?

37

Nature Calls

A HEARTFELT
AND HUMBLING PLEA
FROM THE BEAUTIFUL
BUMBLING BEE
AND IT'S FANCIFUL FLIGHT
IN THE PERILOUS PLIGHT
OF THE REALM OF THE
FLOWER AND
TREE.

40

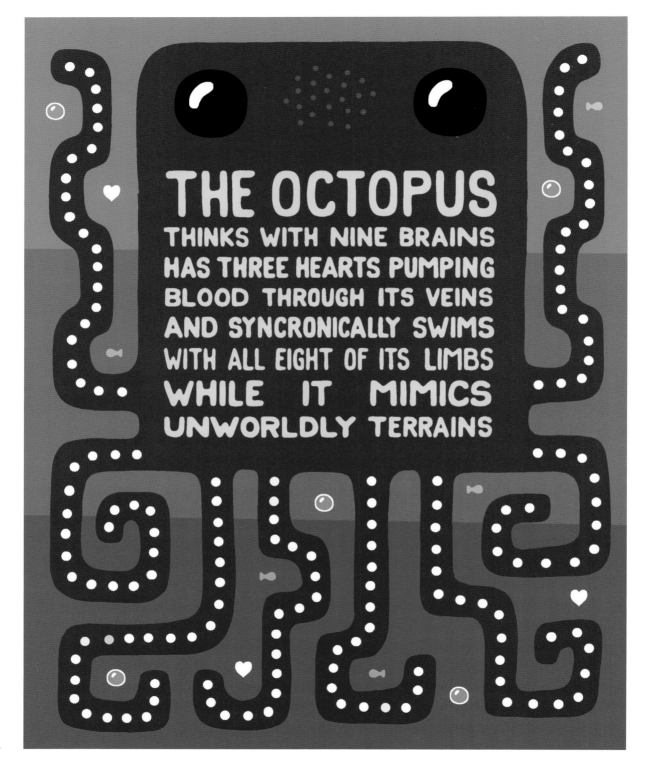

THE OCTOPUS
THINKS WITH NINE BRAINS
HAS THREE HEARTS PUMPING
BLOOD THROUGH ITS VEINS
AND SYNCRONICALLY SWIMS
WITH ALL EIGHT OF ITS LIMBS
WHILE IT MIMICS
UNWORLDLY TERRAINS

THE
MAGNIFICENCE
OF OUR MINDS
UNBOUND BY THEIR
MORTAL CONFINES
FOREVER UNFURLED
OUT INTO THE WORLD
SO BEAUTIFULLY
INTERTWINED

For the Love of Words

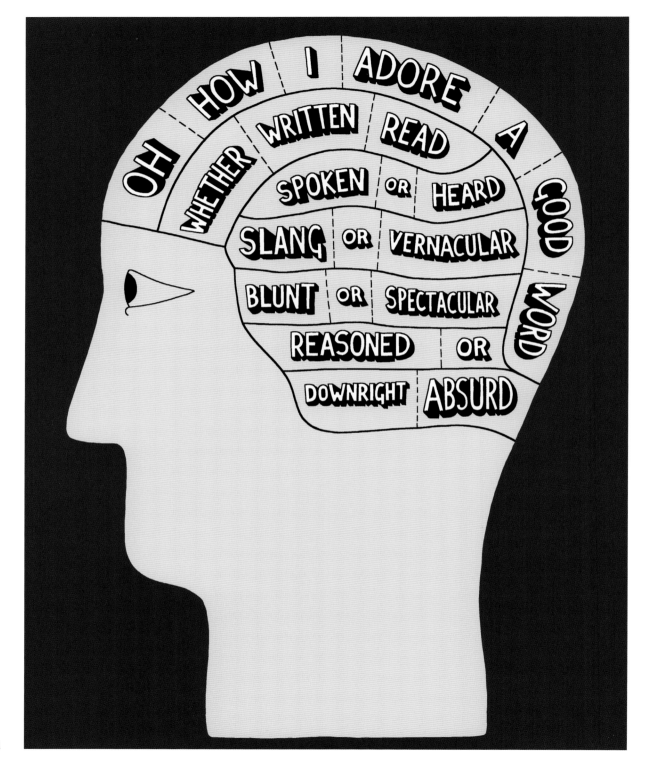

WHEN TRYING TO WRITE
FROM THE HEART,
IT'S HARD TO KNOW
WHERE TO START
MORE EASY, I FIND
TO WRITE FROM MY

MIND

AND TRUST THAT
MY ♡ FEELINGS
IMPART

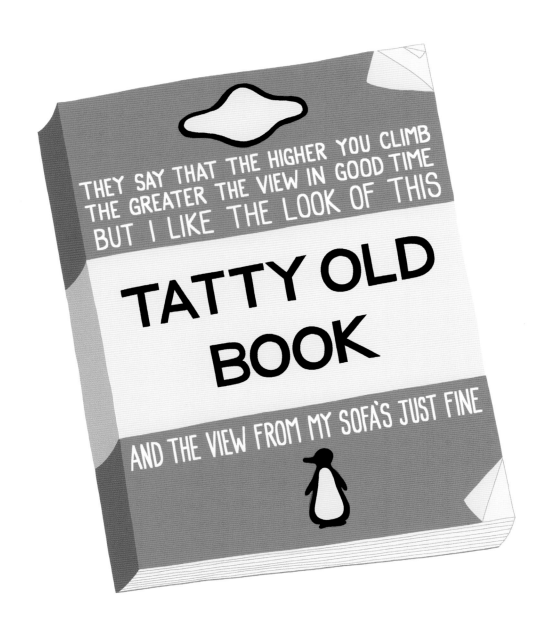

THEY SAY THAT THE HIGHER YOU CLIMB
THE GREATER THE VIEW IN GOOD TIME
BUT I LIKE THE LOOK OF THIS

TATTY OLD
BOOK

AND THE VIEW FROM MY SOFA'S JUST FINE

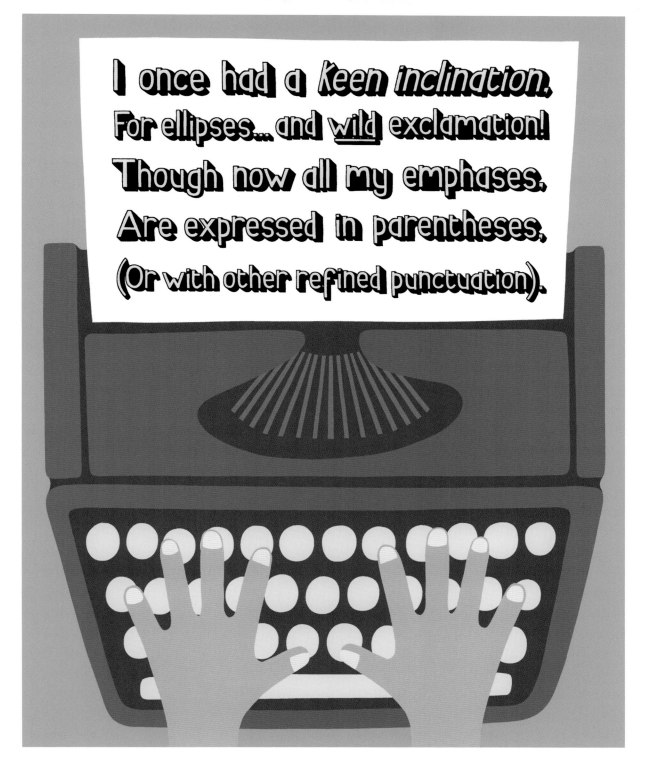

Food, Glorious Food!

HAPPY
FOR YOU TO DECIDE
IF THEY'RE
POACHED, SOFT-BOILED, OR FRIED
BUT THERE AIN'T NOTHING FUNNY 'BOUT
YOLK
THAT AIN'T RUNNY
IT'S ONE THING
I CANNOT ABIDE

WHEN
LIFE GIVES YOU
LEMONS
TAKE HEART – MAKE A FRESH
BUTTER PASTRY, TO START.
SUGAR CREAM WITH A WHISK
FOLD IN EGGS, DOUBLE-BRISK
ET VOILA! YOU'VE A
SWEET LEMON
TARTE.

NEVER
IN ALL OF MY DAYS
HAVE I FELT A PARTICULAR PHRASE
DOES MORE FOR THE SOUL THAN
"FANCY A BOWL OF SPAGHETTI
BOLOGNESE?"

IF THEY'RE MODESTLY-BROWNISH AND ROUND, AND THEY'RE BOUND TO BE FOUND IN THE GROUND, PLEASE TELL ME WHY DO I CRY WHEN I TRY TO DENY THEY'RE SO DEEPLY PROFOUND?

I ONCE CAUGHT A MAN
EATING FRIES
IN THE MOST APPETIZING DISGUISE
HE HAD LETTUCE AND BREAD
EITHER SIDE OF HIS HEAD
AND PICKLES TO COVER HIS EYES

THERE ARE PEOPLE WHO ALL WILL ADORE WITH A SWEETNESS THAT'S HARD TO IGNORE...

...AND THEN SOME WHO REVEAL A PERPLEXING APPEAL JUST TO THOSE WHO SEEK OUT THEIR ALLURE.

IN FRANCE
WHEN PRONOUNCING THE WORD
THE LAST CONSONANT SELDOM IS HEARD
YET IN BRITAIN SOME WANT TO PRONOUNCE IT

"CROISSANT"

THEN BEHAVE AS THOUGH NOTHING'S
OCCURRED.

THE INSATIABLE EARL DECLARED, LUNCHEON SHOULD BE PREPARED

HIS SAVOURY TREAT? A PORTION OF MEAT SERVED BETWEEN SLICES OF BREAD.

Here Comes the Science

THE SCIENTIFIC METHOD

QUESTION
RESEARCH
OBSERVATION.
PREDICTION
EXPERIMENTATION.
INITIAL CONFUSION. INSIGHTFUL CONCLUSION.
DISCUSSION REVIEW PUBLICATION.

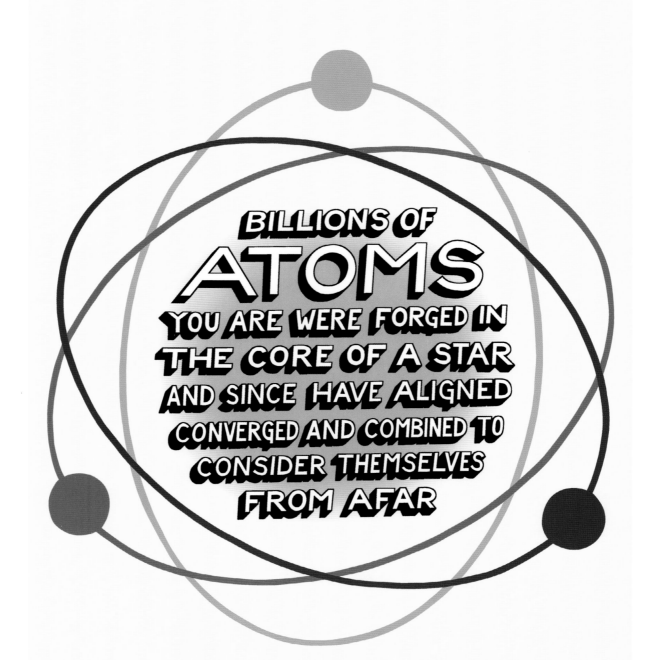

BILLIONS OF
ATOMS
YOU ARE WERE FORGED IN
THE CORE OF A STAR
AND SINCE HAVE ALIGNED
CONVERGED AND COMBINED TO
CONSIDER THEMSELVES
FROM AFAR

IF EVERY FORCE CAN RELY
ON AN EQUAL, OPPOSING REPLY
DID PLANET EARTH BOUNCE
BY EQUAL AMOUNTS
WHEN THE
APPLE
FELL OUT OF
THE SKY?

CALCULATING AVERAGES

FOR THE
MEAN
TAKE THE SUM
OF ALL ENTITIES
THEN DIVIDE IT
BETWEEN THEIR IDENTITIES
FOR THE MEDIAN COUNT
TO THE MIDDLE AMOUNT
FOR THE MODE
FIND THE ONE WITH MOST PLENTITIES

CONVECTION ↑

WHEN PARTICLES RACE
HEATING UP
AND ALL OVER THE PLACE.

CONDUCTION ⇨

DIRECT WHEN THE OBJECTS CONNECT.

RADIATION ⬇

THIS TRAVELS THROUGH SPACE.

79

PERPETUAL MAGNIFICATION
OF A LINEAR VISUALISATION
IN EVERY FORM ANOTHER IS BORN WITH
IDENTICAL CONFIGURATION

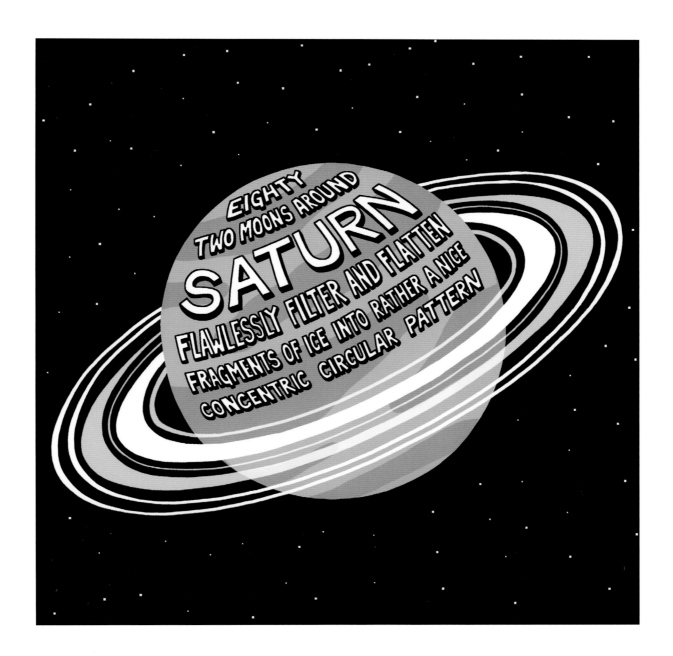

FOUND
WITHIN EVERY CELL
IS A BIOSYMMETRICAL SPELL
A BEAUTIFUL ODE
OF GENOMIC CODE
TO CONJURE UP THIS
MORTAL SHELL

OH WHAT A
MARVELOUS MIND!
THE GENIUS, ALBERT
einstein

HOW HE GOT IT RIGHT
SHOWING MATTER AND LIGHT
THROUGH SPACE
IN A FABRIC
WITH TIME.

THE UNIVERSE
TRULY DEFIES · OUR DESIRE
TO · IMAGINE ITS SIZE
THERE ARE TRILLIONS OF STARS
LIKE THE STAR WE CALL OURS
WITHIN EACH TINY PATCH
OF OUR SKIES

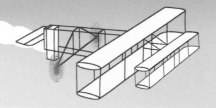

ORVILLE
AND WILBUR WRIGHT
SUSPENDED IN AWE
AND DELIGHT, WHEN THEIR
PROPELLOR PLANE
WAS THE FIRST TO SUSTAIN
A PILOT IN MOTORIZED
FLIGHT

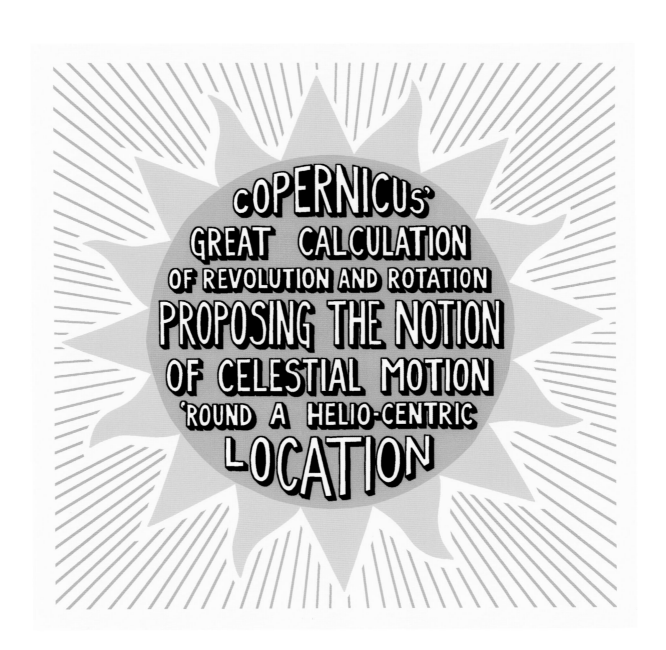

cOPERNICUs' GREAT CALCULATION OF REVOLUTION AND ROTATION PROPOSING THE NOTION OF CELESTIAL MOTION 'ROUND A HELIO-CENTRIC LOCATION

I SIT LOOKING SKYWARDLY GAZING
AND MARVEL HOW LIFE IS
AMAZING

THEY SAY IT BEGAN
WITH A MIGHTY BIG BANG
NOW WE'VE ALL GOT
DOUBLE · GLAZING

MASLOW'S

HIERARCHY OF NEEDS

IS A FRAMEWORK
BY WHICH ONE PROCEEDS

FROM WHAT NATURE REQUIRES
TO ONES GREATEST DESIRES

THROUGH A LOGICAL SERIES OF DEEDS

OUR NATURAL PREDISPOSITION
FOR PATTERN AND FORM
RECOGNITION
IS THE REASON
OUR MINDS
ARE
ALL TOO
INCLINED
TO CONCEIVE AND BELIEVE
SUPERSTITION

Arty Ones

AT FIRST, HE EXPLORED THE
SUBJECTIVE
BUT THE ARTWORLD
REMAINED UNRECEPTIVE
NOW HE SPENDS HIS TIME
ON NONSENSICAL RHYME
HE'S BEEN OFFERED A
TATE RETROSPECTIVE

AN ELDERLY HENRI MATISSE

CRINKLED AND CRUMPLED AND CREASED

THIS GRAND PAPER TRAIL, ONE WONDERFUL SNAIL.

HIS MOST REMARKABLE PIECE,

WARHOL'S UNIQUE RECOGNITION
OF OUR MODERN DAY
HUMAN CONDITION
THE COLOURS AND LINES
OF COMMERCIAL DESIGNS
ALL IN ENDLESSLY SLEEK
REPETITION

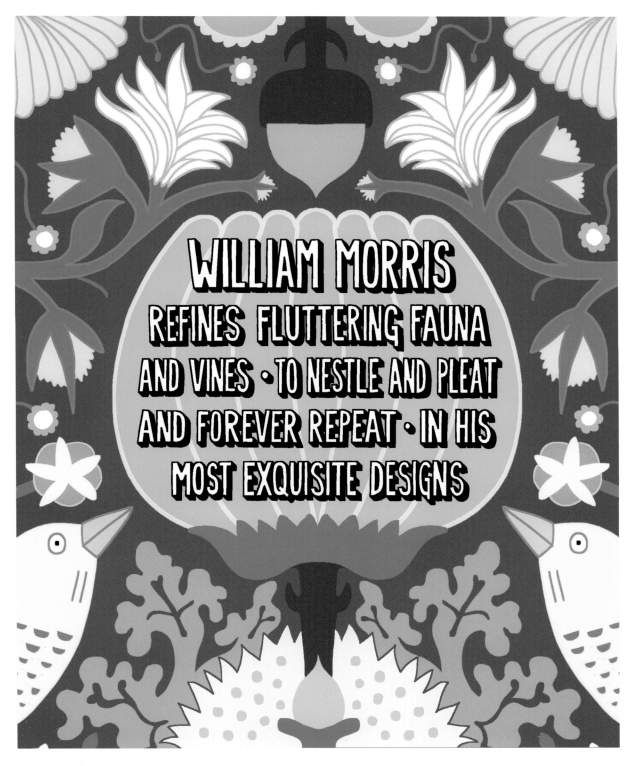

WILLIAM MORRIS
REFINES FLUTTERING FAUNA
AND VINES · TO NESTLE AND PLEAT
AND FOREVER REPEAT · IN HIS
MOST EXQUISITE DESIGNS

MOZART
WOULD CLAIM, SO IT'S SAID
HE COULD WRITE
SYMPHONIES
IN HIS HEAD
BUT, FAR AS
WE KNOW OF
HE WAS RATHER
A SHOW-OFF
AND PREFERRED
PLAYING LOUDLY
INSTEAD.

Modern Life is Rubbish

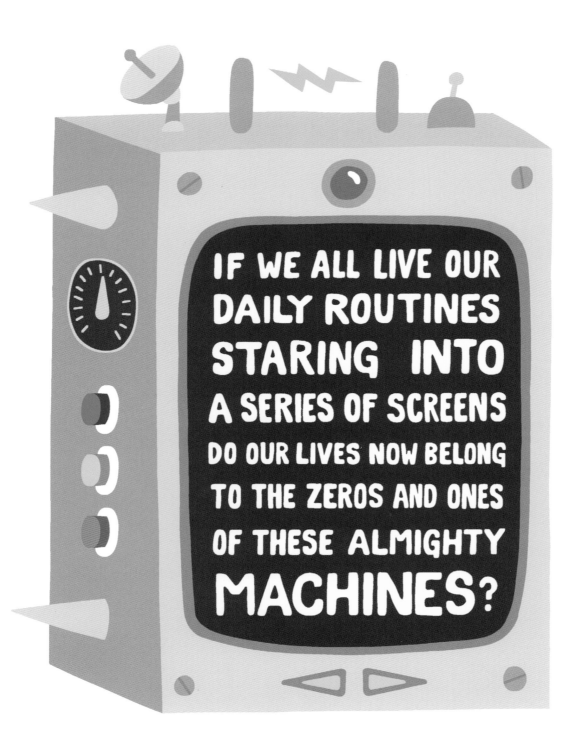

IF WE ALL LIVE OUR DAILY ROUTINES STARING INTO A SERIES OF SCREENS DO OUR LIVES NOW BELONG TO THE ZEROS AND ONES OF THESE ALMIGHTY MACHINES?

EURO-SKEPTIC NIGEL FARAGE WANTED A BRAND-NEW VISAGE SO HE THREW HIS GILLETTE DANS LA TOILETTE AND GREW AN OUTRAGEOUS MOUSTACHE

IT'S A SAD SORRY STATE OF AFFAIRS
WHEN THE *GREAT* BRITISH TABLOID DECLARES:

NATION'S DISLIKE OF THE UNION STRIKE!

But the workers? Well... nobody cares.

The Old Codgers

I MET AN OLD CODGER NAMED FRED
WITH A SINGLE GREY HAIR ON HIS HEAD
I SAID "JUST YOUR LUCK, THAT. WHY DON'T YOU PLUCK THAT?"
HE SAID "NAH MATE, I'LL DYE IT INSTEAD."

A CANTANKEROUS
MAN FROM CARLISLE
SOLD LIQUORICE LACE BY THE MILE
I SAID "THAT'S ECCENTRIC,
WHY DON'T YOU GO METRIC?"
HE SAID "KILOMETRES
AIN'T WORTH MY WHILE."

Soppy Ones

A PERFECTLY CUTE LITTLE NOSE AND THE TINIEST DELICATE TOES. INDESCRIBABLE JOY FOR OUR NEW BABY BOY AND A LIFETIME OF LOVE, I SUPPOSE.

WHAT IS L🍓VE? CAN WE KNOW THAT IT'S TRUE? AND DO I FEEL THE SAME WAY AS YOU? LET US SHOW IT EACH DAY IN THE SIMPLEST WAY WITH EACH SWEET LITTLE THING THAT WE DO

The Odd Ones Out

THE BOXER, MUHAMMAD
ALI
WAS OFTEN MISQUOTED
YOU SEE... I'VE GOT
THIS HUNCH, THE STING
OF HIS PUNCH
WAS MORE LIKE THE
STING WHEN I
PEE.

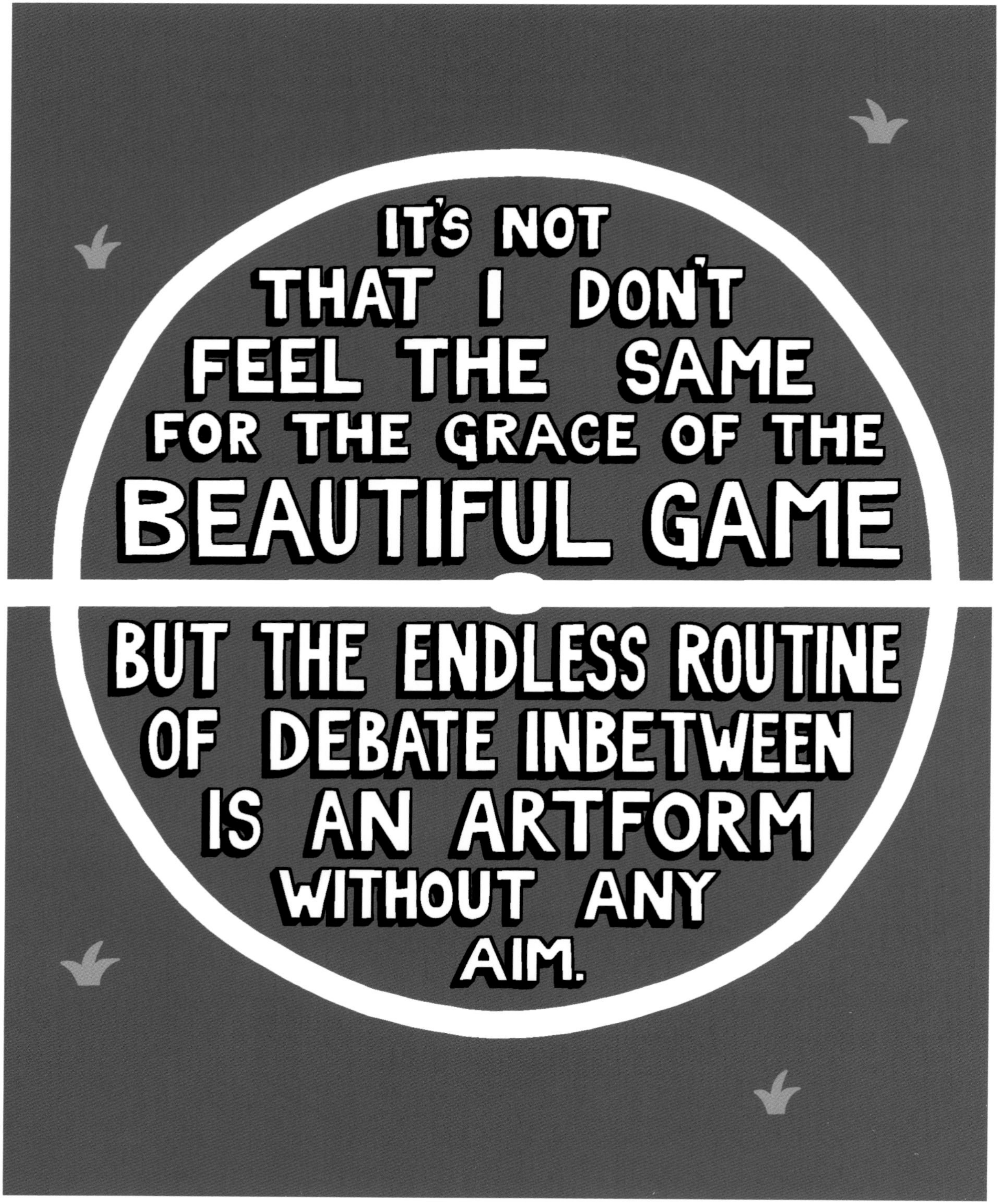
IT'S NOT THAT I DON'T FEEL THE SAME FOR THE GRACE OF THE BEAUTIFUL GAME
BUT THE ENDLESS ROUTINE OF DEBATE INBETWEEN IS AN ARTFORM WITHOUT ANY AIM.

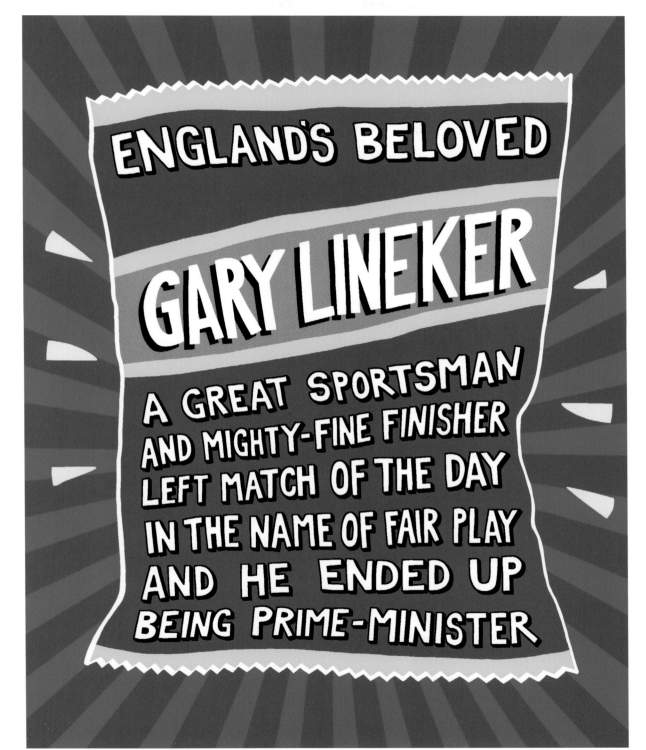

I'VE HEARD THAT THE FEMALE MEMBRANEOUS
IS FOND OF BEHAVIOUR
SPONTANEOUS
SO NOW AT FIRST GLANCE
I PEE IN MY PANTS
AND CARTWHEEL AROUND
SIMULTANEOUS

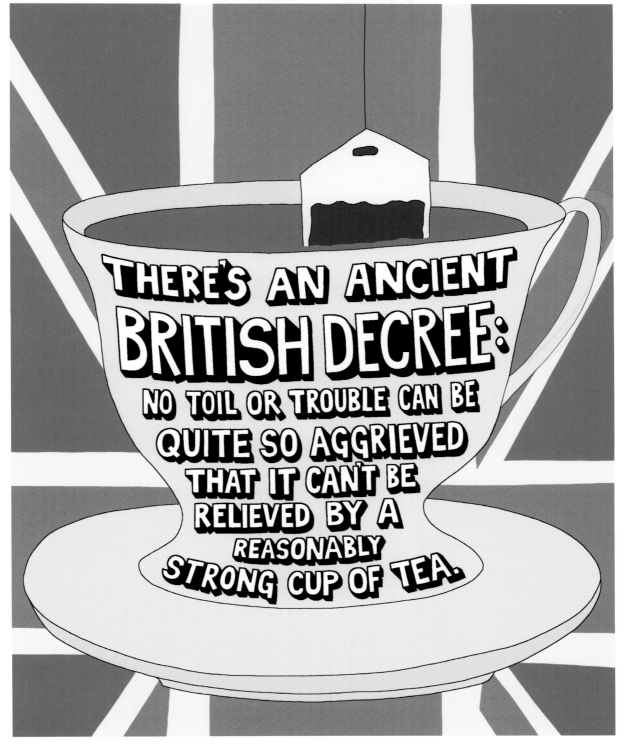

ADVENTURE THROUGH GREAT BRITISH SCENERY THE BUSTLING TOWNS AND THE GREENERY THE CLICKETY-CLACK OF THE WHEELS ON THE TRACK AND THE RUMBLE OF HEAVY MACHINERY

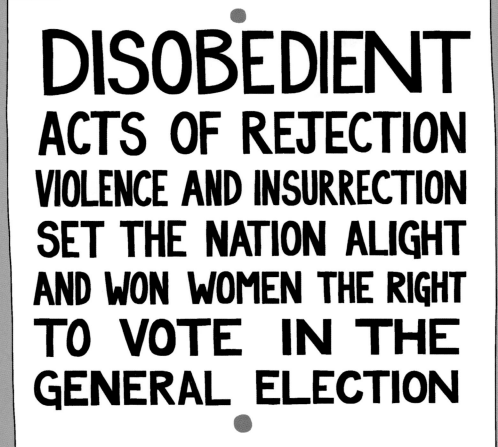

THE STRANGE
ILLUSTRATOR WITHIN
LIES AWAKE THROUGH
THE NIGHT WITH A GRIN
AND HE DRAWS WHAT HE THINKS IN

INVISIBLE INKS

THEN THROWS IT ALL
INTO THE BIN.

Clerihews About Artists

A clerihew is a four-line verse with an AABB rhyme structure. They are biographical, with the subject's name taking up the first line. They are typically whimsical, frequently absurd, and the rhymes are often forced. The form was invented by the English writer, Edmund Clerihew Bentley (b. 1875) while he was a pupil at St Paul's School, London.

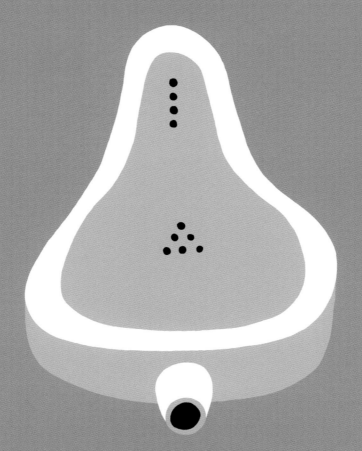

MARCEL DUCHAMP
TURNED HIS SCHOOL
INTO A SWAMP

'CAUSE HE ENTERED THE URINAL
IN HIS ART DEGREE FINAL

RENÉ MAGRITTE
WHAT A HYPNAGOGIC TREAT

BUT DON'T BELIEVE HYPE
IT REALLY WAS A PIPE

CLAUDE MONET
WASN'T VERY FUNNY

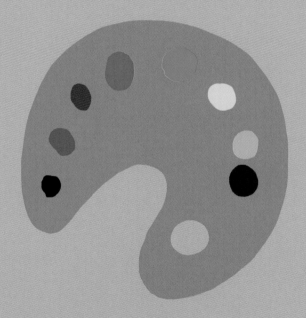

BUT HE MADE A GOOD IMPRESSION

IN A SERIOUS PROFESSION

EDVARD MUNCH
HAD A TERRIFYING HUNCH
SO HE DREW A LITTLE SQUIDGE
OF A MAN ON A BRIDGE

MARK ROTHKO
WHAT A WASTE OF CLOTH THOUGH

ONLY TWO COLOURS
AND HE ALWAYS CHOSE THE DULLEST

DAMIEN HIRST
IMMERSED

A POOR LITTLE CALF
THAT HE CHOPPED IN HALF

Other Curiosities

If You Try Every Day

If you try every day in the spirit of play,
To write just a verse, free-of-thought,
You curious mind will soon be inclined,
To discover what cannot be taught,
For every word ever written or heard,
Was once entirely new,
They come from a place deep inside all of us,
It's here inside of you too.

If you try every day in the spirit of play,
To make just a small work of art,
Your curious hands will soon understand,
How to follow the will of your heart,
Then everything that you feel inside,
As you gaze at your subject and think,
Will forever be there, in the smudges and lines,
Of your paint, pencil, charcoal, and ink.

Pigeons Are Disgusting

Pigeons are disgusting,
They're rats with wings,
They hobble on their stumps,
They eat food out of bins.

But what if I told you,
That a pigeon is a dove,
The universal symbol,
Of hope, peace, and love.

The only difference being,
These pigeons live in towns,
'Til their bright white feathers,
Turned a mucky grey brown.

So next time you see a pigeon,
And you feel no affection,
Remember that you're hating,
On your own reflection.

Poem For A Supermarket Advert

Here's to chips in crusty rolls, pancake stacks, toad-in-the-hole,
Here's to gooey cheese fondue, suet dumplings, winter stew,
Here's to hearty bolognese, carrots with a honey glaze,
Here's to perfect Sunday roasts, here's to humble beans on toast,
Here's to pie and here's to mash, here's to chocolate ganache,
Here's to cupcakes and eclairs, haute cuisine, and tear-and-shares,
Here's to sitting down with mates, here's to all those empty plates,
Here's to one last little treat, here's to... you know what? Let's eat.

If Drinking Makes Me Angry

If drinking makes me angry,
And sugar makes me weak,
If dairy slows me down,
And bread will ruin my physique,
If romance makes me crazy,
And money makes me sad,
Why must it feel so good to be so very, very bad?

Haiku

Just because something,
Is written as a haiku,
Doesn't make it deep.

Leisure

What is this life if, full of care,
We have no time to like and share?

No time to scroll from head to footer,
And spend all day on our computer.

No time to read, when words we pass,
Through keyboard, mouse, or touchscreen glass.

No swiping right, by dim backlight,
On future lovers in the night.

No time to stumble on, by chance,
Embedded gifs where pixels dance.

No time for plays, or tweets, or pokes,
Nor clickbait links, or viral hoax.

A poor life this if, full of care,
We have no time to like and share.

With apologies to WH Davies

My Brain Is Like An Old Computer

My brain is like an old computer... clunk... bleep... hum.
Once that little light turns on all hope of sleep is done.
The operating system counts the memory on the screen,
An out-of-date tradition from an out-of-date machine.

The background changes colour, darker grey to lighter blue,
So I give my mouse a wiggle, tap on the space bar too,
As the applications load across the cathode-ray display,
A smattering of pop-up windows gather in the way.

The first one says the clock's reset, what's the date and time?
The second says my hard drive's full, some files are offline,
The third one says the latest software update's overdue,
The fourth one is an unknown error, haven't got a clue.

But I've seen all of these warning signs too many times before,
So do the same as yesterday, press cancel and ignore,
I know I can't ignore the faulty wiring in my brain,
Though I don't know what to do but turn it off and on again.

Acknowledgements

Firstly, thank you to everyone who has ever bought a piece of my artwork. Publishing this book myself only seemed like a good idea because of your continued support.

Thanks to everyone who has ever commissioned a mural, exhibited my work, published an article about me, given me paint, lent me equipment, helped me with funding applications, taken photos or filmed me working, or helped out in any way. Goodwill is a lovely thing and I feel like I've benefitted from more than my fair share over the last 7 years.

A huge thank you to all my friends, and to my wife, Alice, for everything.

Photo by Stuart Walker - page 5
Photo by Ben Katzler - page 8
Photo by Leila Jones - page 160
Photo by London in 360 - page 161

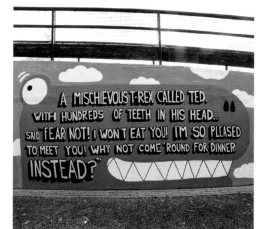

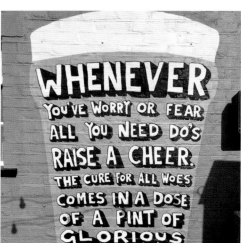

ALL THAT WE'VE GOT IS THIS PALE BLUE DOT.

ANGRY DAN

A PROSPEROUS PIRATE NAMED JADE
TOOK HER CHEST OF GOLD COINS AND A SPADE
SHE BURIED HER TREASURE LIKE A LADY OF LEISURE
UNDER NEW BRIGHTON PARADE

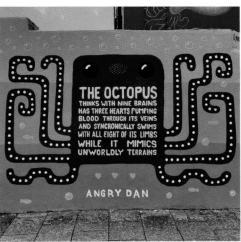

THE OCTOPUS
THINKS WITH NINE BRAINS
HAS THREE HEARTS PUMPING
BLOOD THROUGH ITS VEINS
AND SYNCRONICALLY SWIMS
WITH ALL EIGHT OF ITS LIMBS
WHILE IT MIMICS
UNWORLDLY TERRAINS

ANGRY DAN

WHY WOULD YOU
WANT TO SET SAIL
ONLY TO HUNT AND IMPALE
A PERFECTLY INNOCENT
NOBLE MAGNIFICENT
BEAUTIFUL BULBOUS
BLUE WHALE ?

J.K. STARLEY
REVEALS HIS VISION
OF LIFE ON TWO WHEELS
THE PEOPLE - ALIKE - CAN ALL
RIDE A BIKE AND SOON
WE'LL BE HEAD
OVER HEELS

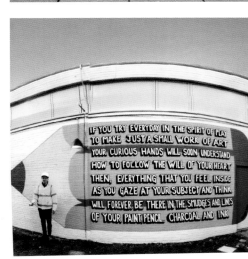

IF YOU TRY EVERYDAY IN THE SPIRIT OF PLAY
TO MAKE JUST A SMALL WORK OF ART
YOUR CURIOUS HANDS WILL SOON UNDERSTAND
HOW TO FOLLOW THE WILL OF YOUR HEART
THEN, EVERYTHING THAT YOU FEEL INSIDE
AS YOU GAZE AT YOUR SUBJECT AND THINK,
WILL FOREVER BE THERE IN THE SMUDGES AND LINES
OF YOUR PAINT, PENCIL, CHARCOAL AND INK

ANGRY DAN'S AMAZING WORLD OF LIMERICKS

LIMERICK
WRITING
COMPETITION